Maximum thrill

It is summer and it is hot.
We are at the Splish and
Splash Park.

Mum, Nat and Dad set up a good picnic spot. Sam and I are off!

There are lots of pools and so much to do. Sam is keen to go on Killer Drop. I'm not so keen.

I get Sam to go with me
to test out the surfing
pool. It was fun.

When Sam yells, "Next up,
Killer Drop!" I look up at
the tower and I feel sick.

I get Sam to come with
me to River Drift. We jump
on, sit back and set off.

Then Sam's pink ring sinks. He tells me, "I think this needs some air!"

We swim for a bit and then
Sam drags me to Killer Drop.

Sam yells, "Look! It's a maximum thrill level. So cool!"

10

We go up the steps to the tower. I am dragging my feet. Sam is running.

Next thing, we are at the top and we are off! Big splashes, big drops, twists and turns. Max thrill!

At the end, I jump up and
tell Sam, "That was the
best! Let's get back on."

Sam looks unwell. He tells me, "No! That was dull. Let's go to Kid Kingdom."

We get to Kid Kingdom
and hop under the full
tipping bucket with Nat.

16

Words to blend

good	pools	cool
park	Killer	tower
keen	feel	needs
surfing	air	thrill
steps	splish	splash
twists	spot	next
drags	swim	spills

Before reading

Synopsis: The family are at the Splish and Splash Park. Sam and Dan go on all the rides, though they find that some are more fun than others.

Review graphemes/phonemes: oo oo ar er ee ur air

Story discussion: Look at the cover and read the title together. Ask: *Where do you think this story is set? Have you ever been to a water park like this? What do you think might happen in this story?*

Link to prior learning: Display a word with adjacent consonants from the story, e.g. *splash*. Ask children to put a dot under each single-letter grapheme (*s, p, l, a*) and a line under the digraph (*sh*). Model, if necessary, how to sound out and blend the adjacent consonants together to read the word. Repeat with another word from the story, e.g. *dragging*, and encourage children to sound out and blend the word independently.

Vocabulary check: maximum – at the highest level; most

Decoding practice: Make cards with the words *thrill, spot, twist, best, drift*. Display them one by one and encourage children to read them as fluently and swiftly as possible, sounding out and blending only if necessary.

Tricky word practice: Display the word *come*. Identify the tricky bit – the o-e, which makes the sound /u/. Practise reading and spelling the word.

After reading

Apply learning: Ask: *Who ended up enjoying Killer Drop? Who didn't enjoy it? Did this surprise you?* Check that children have spotted that Sam and Dan each end up changing their mind about this.

Comprehension

- Where did the family go for a day out?
- What did Dan and Sam go on first?
- Which did Sam enjoy more – Killer Drop or Kid Kingdom?

Fluency

- Pick a page that most of the group read quite easily. Ask them to reread it with pace and expression. Model how to do this if necessary.
- Encourage children to read Sam's words on page 10, with as much expression as they can.
- Practise reading the words on page 17.

Tricky words review

we	are	the
there	when	so
do	me	out
he	my	was
I'm	come	for